Verses

Versus

Verses

Kevin McCormack

Thank you for purchasing *'Verses Versus Verses'*, my first ever published poetry collection. Will there be another? Who knows. I am a firm believer though that life is improvised, and so, I generally like to go with the flow - and right now, at this moment in time, it feels right for me to put at least this much of what I have written between these covers.

This collection is a goulash of pieces from different times in my life, some of which were penned by previous incarnations of the man I am today. When reading through the earlier poems for selection for inclusion in this collection, they threw up many memories - some good, some not so – reminding me of both happy times, and the darkest days of my struggle with my own mental well-being.

The themes in this collection are varied – hence the title – *'Verses Versus Verses'*. Some of what I write is written with my mindfulness and meditation teacher's hat on and carries messages of hope, assurance and acceptance.

The very first poem in this book is one such poem- a piece called *'If This Time'* (penned towards the end of lockdown in May 2020), the reaction to which (pretty much worldwide) has given me the courage to finally put this book together. It's the lengthiest piece I've ever written, as, I guess, when I sat down to write it, I had a lot to say. I owe a lot to *If This Time*, as it has opened many new avenues for me, and connected me to people with whom I know I will have life-long ties; and so, I felt it only fitting to let it fill the first few pages of my first ever poetry book.

Some pieces have been inspired by the life stories of some of the many interesting people I have met over the years, whether it was through day to day acquaintance, or through my time as an actor - a trade in which the observation of others is a key tool in informing the creative process. More verses are very personal to me, finding their voice in the recesses of my childhood, as well as in my current and closest relationships.

I've also added a few pieces which grew from some of the random ramblings and musings that enter my head in the small hours of sleeplessness, or surfaced as a creative response to what's dark and dirty about this world.

So yes, what you've got in your hands is a fairly eclectic mix.

Whatever inspired them, or whenever, these poems are all from that creative corner of my heart, that place of expression that exists in us all, and sadly lies dormant in most.

My greatest wish for you as you thumb through these pages, is that you will heed any urge in you, however slight, to put pen to paper and write some poetry of your own. Who knows, you too may even take the plunge and publish a collection someday, and when you do, please be sure to let me know, so I can return the favour and buy your book in return.

I hope you enjoy 'Verses Versus Verses'.

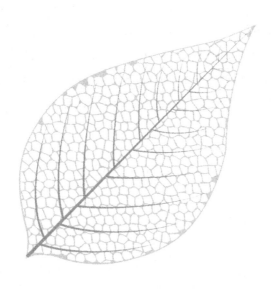

Dedication

This book is dedicated to the people I love, who in turn, make me feel loved. To my mother, Catherine - a woman who reminds me every day that we can only take life as it comes - and that it is in letting go of expectation, we stand some chance at attaining contentment and acceptance.

To my wife, Jacinta – my best friend and soul mate, without whose ongoing love, encouragement and support, I quite literally would not be here today. To my children, Alison and Andrew – two beautiful souls who have taught me more about myself and the world around me than anyone else or anything else ever could. To my siblings, William and Ann-Marie who really have no clue what to make of me half of the time, yet love me regardless.

Kevin McCormack, January 2021

ABOUT THE AUTHOR

Kevin McCormack is a writer, coach, & spoken word artist who lives in Co. Cork, Ireland.

He came to prominence as a poet during 2020 - when he shared recordings of some of his works on YouTube and other social media platforms. His poems from during the late spring of 2020 (when much of the world was in 'lockdown'), continue to resonate far and wide; gaining him a following from as far afield from his native Ireland as South Africa, South America, Australia, New Zealand, U.S.A. and Canada.

Opening with one of his most widely known poems – 'If This Time', 'Verses Versus Verses' is Kevin's first published collection – a selection of widely contrasting pieces which demonstrate his versatility as an up-and-coming purveyor of words and imagery.

'Verses Versus Verses' is also available as an audiobook, voiced by Kevin himself.

Contents

'If This Time'

If this time has taught me anything,
it is that the tiny spec in this universe that we occupy
is both wonderful and wondrous,
and if we allow it to,
the beauty around us
can unlock the beauty within us;
and teach us far more
than our schooling ever did.

If this time has taught me anything,
it is that success
and how we measure it,
needs to be re-defined,
and that the only person
to whom you should ever compare yourself,
is who you were yesterday.
Make your growth-game strong,
and along the way,
be kind to yourself –
if you are doing your best,
you are doing enough.

If this time has taught me anything,
it is that it is more important
now than ever before,
to see the world through your own eyes.
Begin by looking at yourself –
look honestly and gently.
Look inward with compassion and kindness,
and look outward with
humility and appreciation.

If this time has taught me anything,
it is that the opposite of love
is not hate, but fear –
and our greatest fear,
is losing that to which
we have become attached.

Yesterday is heavy,
put it down.
Seeing the beauty in the world around you
is the first step in
purifying and clearing the mind,
and if this time has taught me anything,
it is that nature,

unlike us,
never apologises for her beauty.

If this time has taught me anything,
it is that life *really* is about the journey,
not the destination –
and it must be,
for surely we are not here
merely to reach the destination,
for the destination is death.
Be alive, for after all,
life is all you've got,
and when you pay attention
to the things for which you are grateful,
you soon forget about
what you think you're missing.

If this time has taught me anything,
it is that bitter tears are the quietest,
and on the days
when your head wants to hang low,
it is important that you look up.
Lift your head.
Take it in, and breathe deep,

for while this world
can sometimes be a hard place,
your reality and what you perceive it to be,
are seldom aligned.

If this time has taught me anything,
it is that beauty truly is
in the eye of the beholder.
We can see universes, within universes –
but only when we pay enough attention,
and this is as true
of the nature within us,
as it is of the nature around us.

If this time has taught me anything,
it is this:
If true love conquers everything,
then self-love gives it the fortitude to do so.
Know that you are more than your scars –
know that every wound in you
that has healed along the way
has taught you what it is to fight back;
and to start again from where you are,
with what you've got,

without seeking the approval of others,
and know that self-love is not vanity.

If this time has taught me anything it is this:
HOPE matters, and we cannot live without it.
This time has taught me
that HOPE is not a wish,
nor a desire for things to be different.
It is a course of action,
a combination of mind and heart.
The future can be better
and can be brighter,
and we each have the
power within us to make it so.
There will be challenges to face along the way,
to which there are many solutions.
There is a source of resilience deep within us all.

If this time does not teach us
that time itself is precious,
then we will have missed the lesson.
The lesson that never before
have the past and the future
been so irrelevant,

and that the quest to 'find ourselves'
has been fruitless to now;
only because we've been searching
in all the wrong places.
We are here, we are now.
We are each and every breath we take.
Every day is a gift –
a gift to begin again,
and to grasp with both hands,
the fresh opportunity to learn,
unlearn and re-learn.
If this time……….. is not wasted.

Be the One

Be the one who wakes up thankful
each and every day,
be the one who speaks the truth,
in everything you say,
be the one who comes to terms
with things you cannot change –
though they may at times be hurtful,
challenging, or strange.

Be the one who reaches out,
to lend a helping hand,
be the one who's brave and
bold enough to make a stand,
be the one who's not afraid
to show you really care,
and rise above the parapet
when no one else will dare.

Be the one who shares a smile
with everyone you meet,
be the one who listens well,

yet still remains discreet,
be the one who understands
that every trial is real
and a gentle touch,
a listening ear,
may help someone to heal.

Be the one who comes to love,
as a place to give, not take,
be the one who knows deep down
that a heart can really break,
be the one who shelters love,
from tears and wind and rain,
and knows just as the storm will pass,
so also will the pain.

Be the one to compromise,
when for the greater good,

the one who will apologise,
when you know you really should,
be first to build those bridges back,
be first to start anew,
for friendships only last the course,
if the course laid out is true.

Be the one who'll call a friend,
when you feel grief or pain,
be the one who asks for help,
don't feel you should refrain,
be the one who's not afraid
to say 'I'm not okay',
for someone out there has your back,
they'll guard you in the fray.

Be the who understands
you're just a human being,
breathing, loving, laughing –
hearing, touching, seeing,
accept you're sometimes fragile,
and this doesn't make you weak,
and you can only do your best,
in anything you seek.

Be the one who has the trust
to love yourself enough,
be gentle and forgive yourself,
don't always be so tough,
self-worth can only come from you,
when all is said and done,
if you seek someone who'll love you most,
well, you must be the one.

Don't Look Back

Don't look back in anger,
in fact, don't look back at all,
for the times we look behind us
are the times we'll likely fall,
by all means take the lessons
that you learn along the way,
the past is neither here nor there –
what matters, is today.

Don't look back in anguish,
at the things that you regret,
at something unforgiven
that you feel you can't forget,
try reaching out – extend a hand,
be strong and have your say,
the past is neither here nor there –
what matters, is today.

Don't look back in torment,
at the times you stood accused,
the times your pride was injured,

or you had your ego bruised,
for ego can enslave us,
make us get in our own way,
the past is neither here nor there –
what matters, is today.

Don't look back in sadness,
don't hold on to your grief,
the living tree does not lament
for every withered leaf,
instead it stands reminded,
that all things must decay,
the past is neither here nor there –
what matters, is today.

Don't look back with guilt today,
for the errors of your past,
don't bear the weight upon your soul,
of prior misdeeds amassed,
you're only human after all,
and prone to go astray,
the past is neither here nor there –
what matters, is today.

Don't look back in vengeance,
and don't look back with hate,
for both of these are poisons
that produce a crippling state,
they'll eat you up,
they'll blind your heart,
and steal your joy away,
the past is neither here nor there –
what matters, is today.

Perhaps look back with gratitude,
for while life at times was tough,
you've made it this far,
here you are,
you're you, and you're enough.
Stay steadfast in the here and now,
and keep yourself on track,
for you are certain to de-rail yourself,
when you choose to look back.

Ode to My Washing Machine

My favourite sound that you make
is the little click
that means I can open the door,
and place the basket on the floor,
and once more
retrieve my clothes for drying.

And I'm not lying when I say
that sometimes I want to kick you,
as my patience wanes,
waiting for that click
you seem reluctant to make.

What are we waiting for?
You've already beeped to let me know
you've finished the cycle,
the washing, the rinsing, and the spinning.
I mean, nobody's really winning here?
You're done!

You know you're done,
I know you're done.
There isn't any fun
for either of us in you tagging
another minute on.
For what?

Did the man who assembled you
in the land of Zen,
decide that every now and then,
it would do us both good to pause?

Well let's offer Mr. Moto
a round of applause,
for this non-biological meditation,
this momentary vacation...... it's working.
CLICK

Thank You.

Here We Go Again

She's under the blankets,
lying fetal, facing the wall
as his key turns in the lock.
Out of nowhere, and anticipated -
here we go again.

Trying to force her slumber,
underscored from downstairs
by a symphony of clatters and clangs,
as he fumbles to make a pot of tea
and assemble a cheese sandwich,
first bite all day.

In the room just off the landing,
tiny toes fast asleep, oblivious,
dreaming of puppy dogs and circus clowns,
as a storm brews in the kitchen below.

The ascension begins,
one stair at a time,
laboured breath,

one hand on the bannister,
one against the wall.

A silent prayer,
that tonight's the night he tumbles backwards,
and cracks his skull against the hall table.

The light from the landing fills up the room
as the door swings in,
a full-on brawl against shoes and socks ensues
terminating with the clearing of the top of the
dressing table.

Tiny toes no longer oblivious.

"Are you awake?"

Here we go again.

His Hands Told a Story

His hands told a story.
More than a story of hard work,
and though he hadn't worked in years,
the dirt remained on his fingers and palms –
the same dirt he carried to school
from the age of five
to the day he left at the ripe old age of eleven,
because that's how it was,
'time to earn your keep', he was told –
not that he saw too much of the
inside of the schoolhouse in his time.

His hands told a story.
The black embedded in his finger nails,
also traced his fingerprints,
making them stand out on his hardened skin
like a weather map,
forecasting weather that was not promising.
Interrupted fingerprints –
every score, every blemish
the residue of a lifetime of heavy lifting.

His hands told a story.
The story of how at sixteen
he traded stones and turf for tarmacadam,
cold early mornings,
and an identity crisis that put him
somewhere between a dog and a Blackman,
because that's how it was.
'Time to earn your wage', he was told.

His hands told a story.
The story of a night in Cricklewood,
and a young girl named Teresa from Bansha
who thought his hands too rough,
as he fumbled awkwardly to undo
his innocence and insecurities.
A momentary surge of courage
brought on by six pint bottles of Mackeson's
and the taunts of the lads in the
winkle pickers and Brylcreem.
'Time for me to go', she told him
as she rushed back to her friends
who all giggled and clucked
in a way that reminded him of
the hens his mother kept.

His hands told a story,
his fingers intertwined,
held fast by the mortician's glue,
and the blackness still cutting through
the pallid hue.
They told the story of a life
that should have been more,
should have been better,
and should have filled with people –
his people,
who would have had the benefit
of the big heart with which
he didn't know what to do.

'Time to go', said the man in the morning suit,
to the handful of us that knew him only as Wexford Tom.
I wonder, did Theresa from Bansha
ever think of him?
For as uncomfortable and fleeting
as their brief time together was,
I know he often thought of her.

It's Good to Let Go

"It's good to let go." She said.

"Maybe I can't." He said.

"Try." She said.

"Why?" He said.

"It's good to let go." She said.

"I feel like I'm flying." He said.

"Isn't it good?" She said.

"I hope this feeling never ends!" He said.

"It will." She said.

"When?" He said.

"The moment you hit the ground." She said.

One Day

One day, we will return to this place,
and re-trace the footsteps
we took to make this memory.

We'll park the car on the top road, by the five bar
gate
and follow a trail as embedded in the earth
as the lines on the face of the old woman
who told us how to get here.

Aiming for the gap in the dry stone wall built five
lifetimes ago,
we'll kick up the cowpats baked by the sun as she
would have done,
and not care about the dust on our shoes.

We'll remember the joy of unearthing the brass
buttons
the old lady had concealed in her childhood days,
burying her treasure –
the remnants of the conflict that took her father in
his prime.

One day, we will return to this place,
as filled with sadness as we are today
at not having listened to the stories she so desperately
wanted to tell,
one day.

Ongoing Back Problems

I am vulnerable and that's okay,
I just need to learn to sit with it.
Sit with the child who never new
how to not feel responsible.
Having big boots to fill,
when I could scarcely fill the boots
that were meant to fit me.

I now know that my frame
became strained, distorted
by the weight I felt upon me,
and over the course of time,
it has failed to repair itself…
ongoing back problems,
a steady source of anxiety
that won't let go,
I wish I could have learned at an early age
to bend my knees.

An innocent child,
neither wise nor smart,
too soft, too trusting, too everything.
I need to sit with what occurred and
re-assure myself that no blame lies with me.

Death and Shit Sandwiches

The greedy bastards.
Not a salad sandwich to be had.
I was delayed in getting to the kitchen table.
Too bad.
I got accosted on my way back from the loo,
as you do,
by my mother's friend –
what's her name?
It's a shame.
I can never remember,
is she Mary or Margaret?
It seems all my Mother's friends
are called either Mary or Margaret,
if not Bridget or Bridie.
I've heard her mention a Gertrude as well,
but women of my mother's vintage
with names as exotic as Gertrude
are thin on the ground.
Not too many around.

Anyway, whatever her name is,
the salad sandwiches are gone.
There's any God's amount of plain ham,
plain cheese,
ham and coleslaw,
cheese and coleslaw
and even ham, cheese and coleslaw.
I mean, who in their right mind
puts fuckin' coleslaw in a sandwich?
No one.
That's who.

There's a whole tray of
plain beef in brown bread-
three parts butter to one part beef,
there's no end to my grief-
and you know at first glance
that no one's going to eat them,
not even the herd of fat fuckers from the rugby club,
those friends of my brothers
who ate all of the aforementioned salad sandwiches.

Bad enough that I can't get my head
around the fact that he's gone for good,
and that I'm not sure what his passing means to me –
but I haven't a hope of figuring it all out
if all I'm left with is a hole in my heart
and shit sandwiches.

The Boat

The boat is sinking.
The captain's throat has been cut
and he doesn't even know it-
the crimson red of the turn of his head,
blending into the burning sunset.
Despite the best efforts of
Orion and the Northern star,
there is no land in sight
as the waves roll over each other,
and into the night.

She stares out at the snow –
her front yard, the mountains
and the sky all one wash of white.
Drawing long and deep on her cigarette,
the outer edges of her brow drooping
as she recalls nights by the open fire,
when she arched her back to meet him-
oblivious to the discomfort
of the flagstones beneath her.

This was before he set sail,
on a voyage to God-knows-where.
Now here they are, both lost at sea,
he literally, and she,
afforded the luxury of metaphor.

The Count

Counting down the minutes,
counting down the days,
counting every second,
counting all the ways.
Counting all the blessings,
counting all the woes,
counting all the yeses,
counting all the noes.
Counting all the goodness,
counting all the joy,
counting all the demons,
counting every ruse and ploy.
Counting all the failures,
counting all the wins,
counting my misgivings, and
counting all my sins.

Counting backwards slowly
in a bid to fall asleep,
counting all my heartbeats
as well as counting sheep.

Counting on the kindness
of the beauty by my side,
who is counting on the drugs I take
to help me over-ride,
all the counting that goes through my brain
and keeps me from my rest,
and I know that I can count on her,
and this is why I'm blessed,
and her hand upon my shoulder blade,
her caress it is the fount,
of the ease and peace and comfort
that can help me end the count.

Hard Man

Head to toe in denim,
with his shirt opened
half way down his torso,
he's walking casually,
or more so with a swagger
that says not a single fuck shall be given today.
Don't get in his way,
he's a man on a mission,
there'll be no fishin' for compliments
or small talk from the younger lads
who are all talk and no action,
they haven't got a fraction of the fight
that he's got in his wiry frame,
he's a hard man who made his name
when men were men and women cowered in corners.
Say what you want about wanton destruction,
he learned more by osmosis than instruction
that if you strike first
you seldom come out worst
in a small town like this -
so he's back on the piss,

drowning both secrets and sorrow,
like he did yesterday
and will no doubt tomorrow.

Walking on a Winter's Morning

There is nothing like a walk on a frosty morning
that lets me know I'm alive (and glad to be),
and that all that has been has had to be
and that I am here and now.
Walking into plumes of my own breath,
serves to remind that death
could come at any minute,
so embrace this day
and be glad you're in it,
and the red sky of the morning
that usually spells out warning
provides the most beautiful eyeline,
a humbling, overwhelming skyline
for the hungry birds to pepper.
Forty shades of green
now all one shade of white
having lost their contrast overnight
under a moon so full
you could read a book by its light.
I walk this morning and take it all in,

for it is a matter of time before it rains again,
and whilst on the plus side the birds will be fed,
I shall return to
staying in bed.

There Is a Light

When darkness falls upon you
and you cannot find your way,
when the night time seems relentless
and you struggle through the day,
when the voice inside is on a loop
and cannot be kept quiet,
you must try to remember,
that inside, there is a light.

Inside there is a light that shines,
and though it struggles to break through,
it is the very essence of
the fabric that is you.
Give yourself permission,
allow your light to shine,
take a breath and give yourself
a chance to re-align,
do not heed the voice that says
'give up, lay down and die',
for when that voice says all is lost,
it's telling you a lie.

There's always hope, always a path,
a way of coming through,
a way illuminated, by the light inside of you.

So take a moment, take a breath,
and imagine in your mind,
a swelling light inside of you,
and slowly you will find,
that with each breath that you take in,
this light will grow and grow,
shining outward from your heart
and helping you to know,
that while the darkness sometimes falls,
here's what you need to do
take a breath and fill yourself,
with the light inside of you.

A Convenient Fiction

Who you tell yourself you are
is a convenient fiction,
with or without friction in the narrative
you are your own story,
a figment of your own imagination,
and no amount of cogitation
will re-write what you've already decided to be true,
for your own version of you,
for better or worse
is chapter and verse
an entity of your own making.
Like the child shaking with excitement
when he has convinced himself
he is Spiderman –
maybe, the man whom you've decided
is inside the man you see
in your reflection isn't
actually seeking correction,
but a change of direction,
to a place where he swings from skyscrapers
and other such capers
in a bid to save himself
from his own story.

There's a Cow

There's a cow on the hill,
on the brow of the hill,
as right now on the hill, she lays.
She seems quite content,
as her time is well spent,
it's how she spends most of her days.

In the field down below,
is a farmer, I know,
who is mending a post by a gate,
he's been working these lands,
you can tell by his hands
he's been working from early 'til late.

While the farmer is busy in fields down below,
the cow watches on from on high,
while both listen to bees
and a sweet-smelling breeze,
causes bright summer clouds to roll by.

*Not currently recycled

There's a storm outside,
lids flipped open
in the wind,
what should be held in
is tossed around for all to see,
I try to gather it all up….and fail,
I guess some things
just aren't meant
to be recycled.

To Be a Man

To be a man at this time,
you do not need to be the guy who
kicks in the double doors and stands
silhouetted by a shaft of blinding white light.
You do not need to save the day,
today or any other day –
but do not get in the way
of those who feel they have to.
Let your wisdom be your super-power,
and impart the lessons
of your own hardships and mistakes
upon those who are impressed by you.
Teach, but do not preach.
Offer counsel where appropriate,
and allow it to come
from a place of empathy, not opinion.
Let your shoulders be shoulders to cry on,
and let your strong hands
hold the hands of those
who feel lost or frightened.
The old regime is gone –

the generations of emotionally
castrated men that we knew
are dead and buried –
let them rest,
and know that you are not one of them.
There is a quiet revolution
happening in every man,
a shift in the sands,
and while, at times you may
feel compelled to steady yourself,
don't.
Allow yourself to slide,
and move to one side
to make way for the man you can be.
Be a new brand of super-hero,
safe in the knowledge that
not all heroes wear capes… in fact,
many… wear socks with sandals.

Today We Mourned
You Differently

Today, we mourned you differently –
not in the way we would have liked to
or felt you deserved.
A fettered celebration,
not enough to even begin
to pay tribute to the life you've lived.

Today, we mourned you differently.
The pageantry was sparse,
we had no singer to sing your songs,
and the shoulders
of the fine men you reared were bare –
they would have gladly though sadly
taken your weight with pride,
and carried you to where you now sleep.

Today, we mourned you differently –
your friends and neighbours lined the street –
a noble gesture, but poor substitute
for the squeeze of a shoulder,

an embrace,
and the vice-grip handshakes full of grief,
solidarity and questions.

Today we mourned you differently –
the bare handful of us,
the chosen few, stood around you,
while broad-backed men from the old days
trembled in the distance,
and from a parked car, your brother looked on with
pursed lips
through the condensation.

Today, we mourned you differently.
Sad eyes looked up from where
big hands were holding little hands
that didn't understand-
not that the big hands understood much better.

Today, we mourned you differently,
but this much is true –
you are gone,
but not without a trace,
as you are in every face

you leave behind,
in every imprint of your foot
on the path you so diligently wore
from the rose bushes
to the kitchen door.

Today, we mourned you differently.

The Old Schoolhouse

The old schoolhouse stands forlorn,
cradled in the landscape
of green and gold.
Its cut stone walls, propped up
by the ghosts
of little children with foreheads
rested in forearms
as they count up to twenty.

Ready or not,
what they term progress is coming,
and this beloved edifice
will soon stand idle.
I walk the loose limestone chips,
kicking thistles as I go,
tracing the steps of every game
of 'stuck in the mud'
that was played out like war -
with the victors emerging
from the clouds of raised dust -
dust that merged with their sweat

and slowly caked on their faces
through an afternoon of twelve times tables.

Resting my elbows
atop the stone wall
that once seemed un-scalable,
my eye is drawn to the old gate,
its paint chipped and worn by years of neglect,
weathered by a lifetime of hard winters
since its last touch the caretaker's brush.

Lopsided, propped by a piece of
ridge tile in a rhombus shape.
See? I was paying attention.

Layers of black, white and green hard gloss,
I never knew it as a green gate nor a white gate,
it was always black in my time.
Perhaps in my mother's time
the gate was bright green,
making a bold statement against
the black moss
growing on the steps inside it.
A drizzle descends.

I knew on my way down here,
that the sky had something to say.
I back in under the fuchsia that now fills
half of what was the girls' end of the yard,
It is vibrant and fragrant as it ever was,
refusing to surrender to the onslaught
of brambles and briars
that are attempting to choke and over take it.

There's no one to cut the briars now,
and so the fuchsia fights her own fight.
I've relinquished much of my play time
to many brambles and briars through the years
that have passed since my days in this old place,
and I carry the ghosts of those children,
with their faces pressed against the counting wall.

We Want You To Know

(A eulogy)

We want you to know that we were there,
and that we held your hand and stroked your hair,
and though you may not have been aware
we were with you 'til the end.

We want you to know how much we cried,
serenaded by Big Tom McBride,
full of grief yet full of pride
for all you meant to us.

We want you to know that an ocean away,
there are young hearts that break today,
and they have asked if we will say
you meant the world to them.

We want you to know while now unseen
by the neighbours who knew your day's routine,
that you are somewhere in between
their fondness and their loss.

We want you to know that the garden soil,
is lonesome for your daily toil
and the roses bow in quiet recoil,
it's as though they know you're gone.

We want you to know that if we could,
we would mark this day as we really should,
for your loving nature and all the good
that you selflessly bestowed.

We want you to know those who held you dear
are sad that they cannot be here,
and they will always feel you near
when they remember you.

We want all this, and still there's more
to this grief we've never felt before,
for we shall ne'er see you more,
Gentle Mother.

Ardmore

With her socks in my pocket
and her plimsolls hanging from my fingertips,
I watch as she ambles along the water's edge,
the salt water caressing her bare feet
as the wind at her back
turns her hair inside-out.

She is at her most content,
connected to the moon
that hangs like a hologram
in summer's bright sky.
Her vanishing footprints on the shore
serve as a reminder
that my time with her is temporary.

She turns and walks toward me,
the sea at her back,
the wind now rolling her hair
across her face
like a hijab of brunette,
silver and gold –

and her damp feet
gathering dry sand as she nears.

Her smile says all that needs to be said,
as I take her hand in mine,
and walk her to the car.

Vigour and Grace

I'm walking away from the rubble,
steadfastly into the light,
curiosity as my companion,
on a quest to pursue what is right.

I'm climbing the sheer face of ego,
the line tethered fast to my hope,
the name of my Sherpa is courage,
who is steadily feeding me rope.

I'm diving the depths of perception,
going deeper with each burning breath,
exploring the wreckage of balance,
meditating on meeting my death.

I'm flying through a sunset of insight,
with a cool breeze of trust in my face,
soaring without fear of falling,
suspended by vigour and grace.

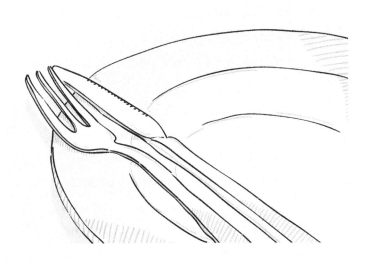

A Balanced Diet

If respect is not on the menu,
I don't want to eat here.
I don't care how much tolerance you're dishing out,
tolerance won't nourish me,
and besides, it gives me wind.

I'm on a strict diet these days and refusing to
consume
platitudes, attitudes and lip service.
This is not a question of pride,
it's just that I've had my fill of side
orders of strained congratulations,
empty calories served on a bed of 'what's
in it for me'?

So, if you're ready to take my order,
I'll have the new season honesty to start,
followed by the medley of trust and faith.
Check back with me about desert,
if there's space, I might chance a slice of regard
and a cup of good will.

Signals

Ascend to the loftiest peak,
light a tall fire and let it speak
from a higher place
than your voice alone can reach,
As the flames dance
against the dead of night -
spewing embers that substitute stars,
let them tell your friends
that you are safe and well,
and your enemies that you are
ready for whatever fresh hell
they can bring.

Let the smouldering embers
write messages of hope
against the dawn's first light,
then lead your rested soul
on the descent into the chaos
that that sent you to higher ground
in the first place.

My Old Addiction

My old addiction is clawing at my back,
digging her nails in deep like a honey bear at a hive.
It's not the most un-natural feeling,
but then, that's what addiction is all about,
I sit in silence, my laboured breath
underscored by the ticking of the wall-clock,
together we are the soundtrack
of a bomb about to go off.
I have little recollection of arriving at this place,
though the aches in my body and
bruises on my soul tell me
the journey was not an easy one.
I breathe deep, and remind myself
that without my scars,
I would have no learning,
and without learning, I would not have
the armoury to cope in this moment.
My old addiction is clawing at my back.

Sepia

(For Frank)

Scattered on the table,
like the pieces of a jigsaw puzzle,
lies a potpourri of Polaroids
and grainy black and white photographs.
I finger through the piles,
my awkwardness causing perished negatives
to crumble like dried flowers.

I apologise to the silhouetted lady
with her jet black face,
in her jet black wedding dress.
Sorry madam, whoever you are,
please forgive me while
I try to discover who I am,
how I got here,
and where the knowing might take me.

A generational mess of times past,
times remembered,
and more times best forgotten by those
begotten of those who went before,
square shouldered men in flat caps,
propped up by the tools of their toil,
men who worked the soil,
pausing for a moment in time
to stand for what would be
the only photograph ever taken of them.

Peering from behind the sepia,
I spot a pair of bright orange bellbottoms,
canopied over a pair of black leather clogs
with scuffed toes.
When was this one taken,
who knows?
The Volkwagen Beetle looks to be as shiny as a new
pin
so If I were to begin to guess
I'd say maybe seventy five,
whenever it was,
Gerard was still alive.
There's one of a young girl in man's boots,

her unblemished face smiling brightly
over the handlebars of a bicycle
which provided all the freedom she needed
in a simpler time,
and I remember her telling of the chime
that told her it was time to cycle to mass.
There's something about old photographs,
snapshots of time that put you
in the places that other people once stood,
connecting, collecting memories,
correcting memories
of someone else's past.

Shore on a Blustery Day

Deep green, swelling, rolling, reaching the edge,
dissolving, returning, hissing,
dissolving on the pebbles.
Driftwood adrift,
arriving on the rocks
as though it has reached
a destination of some sort.
Tall dry grass flattened by a wind
that is just passing through,
headed everywhere and
going nowhere at the same time.
Sand swirling,
cutting curves against
a barely visible horizon,
beautiful yet inconvenient
against a reminder that
there's an outer limit.
A young woman,
leaning and searching,
walks straight past me,
her arm raised across her face

to cover her eyes –
the blind leading the lost,
as her form cuts an interruption
into the manic artwork of the raised sand –
vandalizing the violence of it all
with her beauty.
All of this is temporary,
fleeting, momentary –
the waves, the sand, the wind,
the woman,
and the man composing this verse.

The Tin

(For Michael)

Grandad's Boland's Biscuit tin
had everything, for every job contained within
its four walls -
whether it was nuts or bolts
or washers or springs,
that one square foot
contained all the things
you might need to get stuff mended -
see, he never would accept
that anything's worth had ended.
He would take it apart
with the stealth of open heart surgery,
explore its inner workings
thinking out loud as he went,
"You see? All that's wrong is that that bit is bent."

There was always a great sense of adventure,
on a day when the tin would be heeled right over

on the bench there,
and he and I would finger through
a lifetime of holding onto
'things that might be handy'.
He'd get me to make a row of washers,
in descending size,
starting from the biggest
down to the smallest,
and as I was not the tallest,
I would do so whilst standing
on an up-turned bucket.
"Fuck it anyway", he'd say,
"we have every size bar the size we need.",
Then I'd say, "Yes Grandad, fuck it indeed",
then we'd both laugh out loud
at our naughty swearing,
with neither of us caring -
see, we never got in trouble
as we pottered away in our own little bubble,
away from Mammy and Nana.

Sing

(For Phil)

Sing the song that's yours,
even if the words don't rhyme,
and even if you can't keep time
and the melody goes astray,
sing it out and sing it loud,
and even if you're not,
pretend you're proud
of your masterpiece,
of your one-verse-long song
or your debut swansong,
at least you're singing something.
Sing the song that's yours,
and follow each word as it surges
and always fight the urges
to sing the stories of others,
sing to your sisters and brothers,
to your uncles and aunts
and embrace the chance
to be mortified by their responses.

Sing the song that's yours,
without apology for its sentiment,
sing every word as it's meant,
and let the world take or leave it,
For songwriters like you are thin on the ground,
with your own perspective
and your unique sound,
there's a lot of 'same old' doing the rounds,
so you just stick to being you.

Departed

Stumbling through hollow spaces
she's searching for cordial souls,
with the voices in her head
asking what her heart should do,
her jaded arms reaching out -
reaching for the departed,
while she cannot even find
proof of life within herself.

She knows it well, she's an empty shell,
having given herself fully
to someone who didn't deserve
a hair from her head –
and now she reaches for the dead.

Through the half-light
of what should have been happy ever after,
she wishes she were half right
when through veiled laughter
she watched him slip an encrusted shackle
along her trembling finger.

Long walks at night,
walking with no one to talk to –
separated from the familiar. Agitated.
He couldn't be swayed
and yet she stayed,
tethered to this world by her progeny,
clinging to hope or hopelessness,
she never could tell the difference.

The same songs play
over and over on the radio,
while the mantra of mischance in
her head harmonises,
and life is full of no surprises,
just the day to day to day routine,
unheard and unseen –
and still she reaches for the departed.

In her summer dress,
her hair a mess,
another long walk of laps
around her swamped continuance,
she hopes to find a voice,
that will offer some choice,

other than what she's living -
and giving in,
the departed reach back –
beckoning her towards the edge.

A Simple Man

I'm a simple man who likes simple things.
I like fresh bread and a fresh bed,
but I don't like fresh bread in bed
'cos the crumbs are a hoor to be dealing with.
I like short walks and long talks,
but depending on whose company I'm in,
these can be better the other way around.
I like home-made chips
and rosie-red lips,
but not if the red is from ketchup.

I'm a simple man who likes simple things.
I like sunsets and sunrises,
but I'm not a fan of surprises
as the unexpected can
heighten my anxiety.
I like chancing and romancing
though I'm not a fan of dancing
'cos the more I dance,
the fatter and uglier I become.
I like writing verse,

and even worse,
I enjoy swearing
at current affairs programmes
on the telly –
splurting profanity at the insanity
of this whole fucking circus.

I'm a simple man who likes simple things,
and I am blessed
to have the best
of those around me,
to guide me and ground me,
and keep me reminded that
I've got a hell of a lot more than I haven't.
I like knowing that in all of the going,
all of the struggle
and the to-ing and fro-ing,
that I can just stop,
and get back on top
by simply taking a breath –
the simplest of things
for this simple man.
I'm a simple man,
who likes simple things.

The Blurred Boy

In an out-of-focus photograph,
I'm staring at a blurred boy
who is squinting back at me.
The sun is in his eyes,
giving him the look of someone
who is trying to figure me out
from where he stands
with his back against a window sill.
We continue to stare each other down,
he with the sun in his eyes,
me, listening to the rain against the skylight.
Where did you go?
Blurred little boy in bell-bottoms.
You grew into a blurred man,
who, on the rare occasion he catches a glimpse of
himself,
is still trying to figure himself out.
The picture cannot be re-taken,
a steadier hand cannot be applied,
and so,
the boy remains a blur.

The Pain in My Neck

(For Joanne)

The pain in my neck is a pain in the arse,
and the voices inside are tormenting,
there's a glint in my eye,
but behind every sigh,
there's a rage beyond rage
that's fermenting,
The struggle is real at this moment in time,
to live like I'm calm and serene,
I'm cool as a cucumber,
or raging like Hulk,
and there's space for
fuck all in between.
I'm sick of concurring
and tired of the worrying,
If 'normal' will ever resume,
Fed up with the endless statistics,
and done with the doom and the gloom,
While I know that my story is common,

and a lot of you all feel the same,
It offers me only cold comfort,
when looking for someone to blame.

If This Christmas Brings a Miracle

(Penned in the run up to Christmas 2020)

If this Christmas brings a miracle,
I hope that it is this,
that we all get to share a hug,
a handshake or a kiss,
with beloved friends and family,
the ones whom we hold dear,
and that those who live in foreign lands,
can once again be near.

I hope we get to drink a toast,
to raise a glass or two,
to drink the health of old and young,
"Here's to me, and here's to you",
and "here's to love and living long
and to our life of plenty",
and "here's to better times ahead",
and "good riddance twenty twenty!"

I hope that as we gather in
to prepare the yuletide feast,
that we find a way to share and give
to those who have the least,
and that when we count our blessings,
(as it is the time to do),
that the spirit of the season
will solidly ring true,
for it is in the giving that
the greatest gift is found,
so parcel up your kindness,
and pass it all around.

If this Christmas brings a sadness,
as you set an empty place,
I hope you feel them all around
as you bow your head in grace,
and I hope that in your sadness,
that some comfort you will find,
in knowing that your soul and theirs
will forever be entwined,
for the ties that bind grow tighter –
always at this time of year,
and when you hold them in your heart,
they always will be near.

If this Christmas brings a miracle,
I hope that it is this,
that we still make magic memories
and one day reminisce,
we'll look back and remember
all the challenges we faced,
as families, as countrymen,
as a united human race,
and we'll count our blessings every day,
not just under fairy light,
and ensure that no one stands alone
to face their grief or plight.

If you believe in God above,
or even Santa Claus,
my wish for you is that you find
the magic in a pause,
a twinkling of reflection,
in amidst the Christmas cheer,
a magic Christmas moment,
when suddenly it's clear,
that the greatest gifts we have in life
don't come wrapped in a bow,
but wrapped in the hearts around us,
and the love that makes them glow.

Falling

Being in love with you
doesn't cause me angst, per se,
my greatest challenge stems from
falling in love with you over and over.
Falling for you every morning when you awake,
falling for you every evening when
you return from your day,
falling for you when you kiss me goodnight
or touch my hand,
falling for you in your every smile,
or when you laugh or make me laugh.
For it is in the falling
that the adolescent
in this middle aged frame
wants to impress you,
make you happy,
make you his.
It is in the falling
that the fear of losing you grows,
caught in a bitter-sweet waltz
of love and logic.

A Quiet Hero

A quiet hero,
he sits in silence
by the stillness of the lake,
watching the reflection
of the sky on
its planed surface.

He has never asked for much,
and his greatest joy
is found in serving others.

His torment,
he keeps to himself,
but comes to this place
to breathe it out.

He seeks no company
on days like this,
other than the
uninterrupted presence
of his true self.

Looking outward
with yearning
at the horizon,
looking inward -
with contempt for
the child inside.

Afloat

(For Kate)

No one saw it coming,
no one was prepared,
no one seemed to care much,
not even those who cared,
no one had the foresight
to rearrange the sails,
now everyone is hanging on
by their teeth and nails.

No one battened down the hatches,
so the cargo is afloat,
it's not just brine, but posturing
that's going to sink this boat,
it's gone too late for mutiny,
it's gone too late to talk,
no time for reconciling
these men of cheese and chalk.

Un-necessary conflict,
the hull awash with pride,
a helpless, hapless, hopeless crew,
their souls all cast aside,
there isn't a horizon,
there isn't land in sight,
there's only waves and wash and woe,
in this moonless, stormy night.

Anticipating Dawn

I'm on my second cup of coffee
and I've not awoken yet,
I'm struggling to remember
all I'm hoping to forget.
I'm staring at the skyline,
anticipating dawn,
there isn't much to stare at
from my perch upon the lawn.
Perhaps I should be sleeping still,
perhaps it would be best
for me to climb to stairs again,
to try resume my rest-
but these verses will not write themselves,
these thoughts demand attention,
and other things that fill my head,
which I feel I cannot mention.
So, here I sit, a true misfit,
the ultimate pretender,
A scrambled mind, the kind you find
when a brain's put in a blender.
I'm done with anger,

done with fear,
I've had my fill of crying,
I'm done with hiding what I've lived,
and from now on I'll be trying,
to let it out, to give release
to the cipher from my youth,
so the ten year old inside of me
will get to speak his truth.

Bridges

Do not kneel,
wailing at bridges that are burning,
do not give into yearning
for things that have
passed for a reason,
don't commit that treason
against yourself.

Do not stand
knocking at closed doors,
or mopping spilt milk from floors
that have opened up
and swallowed you.
Walk away from
the version of you
who has followed you
to this place of change,
all of this has happened
so you can rearrange-
make better choices,
hear new voices,

broaden your thinking
and horizons.

Get your shit together -
there's a change in the weather,
and your history
has gifted you
all the shelter you need.

Donations in Lieu

Don't become a statistic,
I mean let's be realistic,
when you rush to timeless slumber,
you become another number -
a headline, a deadline, for a maths and stats reporter,
who ought to realise
that every number has a name.
And there's no shame
in talking of the dark,
I'd rather see you park up your pride,
take me or anyone else to one side,
and have the balls to say "I'm not okay".

Don't fear the confusion,
or the feeling of intrusion
that you worry might follow,
if you feel compelled to speak,
don't swallow what needs to be said.
Rest your head
on the shoulders of those who've got you
and can see that this is not you,

and are happy to help you carry your load,
or walk with you on a road
that leads to where you are better.

Don't become a statistic,
I mean let's be realistic,
the greatest gift in someone's life is you
and let's not ask for donations in lieu,
and yes it's shit when you don't fit,
but more often than not,
all of those spaces and places
can be flexible,
can be moulded
to a point where you,
once unfolded
can comfortably exist,
and you would be so badly missed.

Halo

Meet me out there,
under the halo of the full moon,
hold my hand
and let our thumbs caress
as we stroll
with crisp white grass underfoot.

Breathe in the silence with me,
inhale the sense
that all of nature is asleep,
bar you and I.

Watch your breath and mine
mingle in the blue light,
the light that serves to remind us
that it is never truly dark.

For this moment,
in this night,
may be all that we have,
and what a moment to savour.

Harvest

(For Fernando)

Come follow me, you weary soul,
and know not all is lost,
and the harvest tethered to your back
will soon be worth the cost
of the bending and the stooping,
and the clawing through the soil,
it's time to claim the dividends
of your hard, essential toil.

It's going to take a day or two
for the backache to subside,
and the dirt beneath your fingernails
will brush away once dried,
the sweat upon your furrowed brow
will soon evaporate,
as the coolness of the evening's air
will cause it to abate.

Your father's father did this work,
your father did it too,
and there never was a question
but one day you'd do it too,
but you have high-hopes for the ones
who follow in your wake,
so you work harder, longer, more,
this cycle for to break.

You earn them opportunity,
and all you were denied,
and watch them flourish,
watch them learn,
and let them see your pride.

The wages of your drudgery,
the payment for your grind,
means that they will never know,
and never be confined
to the daily slog,
'work like a dog' life
you've only ever known -
and thanks to you,
and all you do,
will start a cycle of their own.

Headshots

(For Pauline)

Embrace your face, my friend,
accept every line with gratitude,
live in an attitude of appreciation
for every station you've passed through.

Be thankful for every lesson you've learned
– good and bad –
for every furrow on your smiling face
has been earned.

Do not fret about your age,
for every page you've turned
has added to your story,
the triumphs and losses,
the grief and the glory
have all manifested upon your brow,
and no matter how
you try to resist,

you must know this:
that beauty lies in the eye of the beholder,
we all grow older,
and while what's on the outside
changes and rearranges,
the loving kindness inside of you
remains flawless
to all who
know and love you.

I Held Your Hand

I held your hand as we walked
to the middle of the floor,
in a smoky hall awash with reds
and blues and yellows.
Jim Diamond sang of how
he should have known better,
and whatever of Jim's lament for
how he got it all so wrong,
your hand in mine felt right,
and we danced that night –
me just being me,
and you, just being you.

You held my hand as we walked
by the river,
along the discrepant path
with its tarmac lifted,
shifted by the roots of trees,
there long before the way
was paved for you and me
to walk towards that kiss,

that moment of bliss -
me just being me,
and you, just being you.

I held your hand as you walked
me up the path
and through the front door
where I was met
with half a welcome.
We sat squashed together
in one arm chair for
the ensuing interrogation,
both of us with our arms folded
and,
under cover of puffy denim sleeves
our fingers were secretly intertwined,
and me just being me,
and you just being you.

You held my hand,
and flanked by flowers
and smiling faces
we walked toward the sunshine
of the church yard,

to better places,
holding onto each other for dear life,
finally man and wife,
too young,
but old enough to know
that these hands would fit forever,
me just being me,
and you just being you.

I held your hand as we walked
nervously
down a corridor that would
lead to only hurt,
part you, part me
but not meant to be,
no words could comfort either of us,
but our fingers in a mesh of
grief offered some relief
and held us both up some bit –
me just being me,
and you, just being you.

You held my hand,
through tears of joy,

first a girl and then a boy,
blessed with the testament to our love,
gifts from above –
(well, I don't know about that),
but having other hands to hold
while they needed
us was celestial while it lasted –
us being us, while letting them be them.

And still to this day,
I hold your hand,
and you hold mine,
through walks and talks,
and all is just fine,
what will be will be,
as long as you are still you,
and I'm still me.

Dig

Pick up a shovel and dig deep
and no matter how steep the edges get
keep digging, because the bravery you are
looking for is down there somewhere.
Keep on mining and
keep refining your thinking -
you've been here before
whether you know it or not
and there's a whole lot
of courage within,
it's just been buried
in your hurry to forget
your tribulations and trials.
You may have to dig
for what feels like miles,
but when you unearth what you need
it will feed into your courage and capacity
in a way you never thought possible.

In the Corner Stands a Chair

(For Justin)

In the corner stands a chair,
from where she gave the orders
and offered counsel that was curt
and to the point -
direct, yet well intentioned,
her words were never what you'd term
'loaded with sentiment'.

More throne than armchair,
she ruled the world as she knew it
from where she sat
in her cardigan and slippers,
the cat at her feet,
prostrate in adoration.

She sat me into that chair one time,
to tend to a graze on my knee,
a non-life-threatening injury,

acquired when I missed the edge
of the path on my way back
from the chapel yard,
I was comforted to know
that even though it stung,
it would be better before I got married,
and you know what?
She was right, it healed well
in the decades that passed
to my wedding day.

As the years rolled by,
the chair looked to get bigger,
though in truth,
we knew this was not the case,
as there she sat, ailing and failing,
until one day, the chair was empty.
No more moments of curt counsel,
and the order to
make the sandwiches
on Christmas night, a distant memory.

Now That All the Gods Are Dead

(For Tom)

Now that all the gods are dead,
where do we go from here?
What are we to idolize?
What are we to fear?
However shall we circumvent
the urge to kill and maim?
Or quell the need for forbidden flesh
with neither sin nor shame?

What will we threaten children with,
without indoctrination?
Or teenage boys who've learned the joys
of endless masturbation?
See, the notion of a god or gods,
requires the infantile,
to believe, without the concept,
that life wouldn't be worthwhile.

God needs your lack of self-belief
in order to exist,
and you to wander aimlessly
through imaginary mist,
on a promise of eternity
in a land of milk and honey,
in exchange for your soul,
it's more about control,
than it is about the money.

The frail old men,
the dying breed,
leaning at their alters,
whilst peddling lies
through endless sighs,
from a book of unknown authors.
They know themselves,
the game is up,
the lid can't be un-lifted,
the insidious have been exposed,
and their audience has shifted.

Pillar to Post

You were to be seen and not heard,
lost and hapless
as your old man stacked stones,
and your mother took to the bed.

Weighed down by your over-sized coat,
made all the heavier by soft rain
and thick smoke,
a boyhood of communion
and carbolic soap,
your education lifted
from the cobblestones -
then pillar to post without words -
to a life of donkey work,
danger work and dirty work.
Strong hands
and weak will,
a devil presented in a pristine parquet box
- to the eye a thing of beauty -
inside,
its contents a riddle to this day.

Primroses

She left home three days ago,
and here, she returns,
with the stars burning behind her eyes.

Dancing across the kitchen floor,
the pockets of her apron filled
with promises and primroses.

Turning on one heel,
she whips the blackened kettle
from the top of the stove -
a tango to the cold tap -
and with a flick of her wrist,
she fills it, via the spout.

Then, cupping the old man's face in her hands,
she kisses him firmly on the forehead
and asks: "Tea, Daddy?"

The old man nods a hasty, perplexed 'yes'.
He has no words,
and even if he did have,
he's afraid to speak.

Safely Home

It is important that you know this.
Wherever you are,
whatever is happening for you,
you can always find your way home.
However far away you are,
this heart and these arms are always open.
Whether it be love, or labour,
or even a labour of love
that carries you away,
this light will be on,
to guide you and remind you,
that however or wherever you are,
I'm here.
You are always near,
and distance is a formality -
for whatever it takes,
I will reach out and grasp your hand
until you are safely home.

I may not have a lot to give,
but I live
to know you are safe and content,
and the time I have spent
in making you who you are,
is my greatest investment of all time.

Shame

Bare feet slapping hurriedly
along cold flagstones at night,
running for their lives -
into the dark,
away from the love of God.
Calloused knees and shriveled fingers
working their way away
from their shame,
towards righteousness,
towards unattainable forgiveness,
a true life-sentence.
Victims of collusion
bearing scars of intrusion,
penetrated by the threat of hell –
hell on earth, sinful birth,
tears of pain, sorrowful sobs
into stained mattresses,
lamenting the loss
of their little monsters
wrenched from their wombs
by the brides of Christ.
Amen

The Kitchen Table

(For Imelda)

The kitchen table has been
the site of shake ups,
break ups and make ups,
of brussels sprouts,
and ins and outs.
It has held up losers and winners
and chicken dinners,
and played host to
games of cards and scrabble –
"What do you mean, 'jabble'?
That's not even a real word!"

It has had everything spread
across its top,
from bicycle parts to
stuff from the shop,
and homework and study,
and boots all muddy,
left carelessly by a breathless child.

It has served as the alter
for therapy sessions,
through boom-times
and ensuing recessions,
it has witnessed tears and fears
and through the years
heard ructions of laughter
and the 'happy ever after'
at the end of fairy tale books.

The kitchen table has been
scalded and scratched,
and it's been a lifetime
since it has matched
the chairs that came with the set,
but it is a place
that won't let us forget,
that memories outlive
even the best built furniture.

The Sticks

Are you even living in rural Ireland
if everyone around you doesn't know
every last thing about you?
All your births, deaths and marriages,
your miscarriages
and misdemeanours,
and all the gaps in between those,
willingly fabricated and filled
by those who love to fuel fire.
They'll talk about your cancer,
and how your husband is a chancer,
a lighting bastard and
a pure disaster
on the pitch in his time.

There's a peculiar elation
when they learn you're a relation
of so and so
"and so I was right all along,
I wasn't wrong –
her mother was a cousin of the father

of yerman who drove the digger" –
and it doesn't get any bigger
than knowing that kind of detail.
If they're not talking about someone else,
they have nothing to say,
(except maybe in a roundabout way),
when debating the history of a farm of land,
"and as far as I understand,
it was meant to go to John",
and the conversation around
the doing and dealings of others goes on.
And then, once a week,
all quiet and meek,
line up with their tongues hanging out for
communion bread – the same tongues that will wag
through scant regard for the message
of the lad who bled to death for them,
allegedly.

This Morning

This morning, it's just me, Maya,
a cup of coffee,
and the sound of the rain.
Weighted words
cascading down the pages
while resentful raindrops
hit the skylights.

I choose, in this moment,
to be transported rather than inspired,
with each and every word from her pen
taking me a step further away
from the rubble of Christmas
strewn about me.
A mess of the half opened,
half-eaten, and already half forgotten,
all battling for limited floor space
in the semi-darkness
of the loosely pulled curtains.

I traverse the verse,
leaving my OCD home alone
to deal with the three sets of fairy lights,
all on different settings on the tree.
Wherever else today may take me,
I will have had this quality time
with this beautiful, creative soul,
who, like me, in her time,
doubted every ounce of her ability.

Be Kind

Be kind, and you may find
that it comes back to hit you
between the eyes,
when you come to realise
that what costs nothing,
brings the kind of great fortune
that riches cannot give.

Live in a 'live and let live' kind of way,
this day and every day,
but don't ever be afraid
to have your say.

Be true to yourself –
your best self,
and dig deep enough
to find true compassion,
there's no need to ration
what you have in abundance.

Try it – don't deny it
if the notion takes you,
or picks you up and shakes you
into giving,
for this life you are living
is a once off,
a chance to do good,
not because you think you should,
but because you believe you can.

Untitled

The joy that lights the happy face
as each new day is born,
The song of thrush and meadowlark,
as they greet the summer morn.
The need to seek the answer
in everything we see,
to give of our best effort
however modest it may be.
To be thankful to good fortune
and the members of our race,
whose help and knowledge given,
made for us a place -
to love, to laugh, to sometimes cry
for that is nature's way,
and is as truly certain
as the closing of the day.
When the shadows lengthen,
and the light fades on the sea,
there is just time for one more thought –
"I'm glad it was to be!"

Author's note: This piece is not my own. It was penned in 1995 by my late uncle, Paddy O' Regan. A peculiar genius with whom I was barely acquainted, but to whom I wanted to give the last word. Kevin.

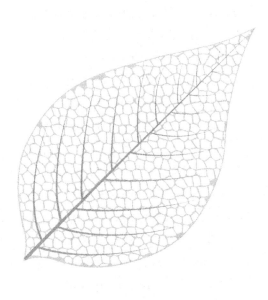

Please Review

Dear Reader,

If you enjoyed this book, would you kindly post a short review on Amazon or Goodreads? Your feedback will make all the difference to getting the word out about this book.

Thank you in advance.

Made in the USA
Coppell, TX
13 June 2021

57373015R00085